THE UNDERGROUND PIONEERS

Victorian London and its first underground railways

Andrew Emmerson

Capital Transport

First published 2000

ISBN 185414 225 9

Published by Capital Transport Publishing,
38 Long Elmes, Harrow Weald, Middlesex

www.capitaltransport.com

Printed by CS Graphics, Singapore

© Andrew Emmerson 2000

ACKNOWLEDGEMENTS

The author would like to thank the following for their help:

John Adams; The late Ken Benest; British Library, Dennis Edwards;
Guildhall Library; Alan A. Jackson; London Transport; Marylebone
Road Reference Library, London; and finally Professor Theo Barker
for his history of London's Transport and the inspiration he gave
many years ago to carry out primary research.

ILLUSTRATION CREDITS

British Library   Pages 8, 18, 27

Guildhall Library, Corporation of London   Pages 10, 11, 26, 33, 36,
   41, 50, 65

London Transport Museum   Front cover, Pages 15, 17, 20, 22, 30,
   31, 32, 33, 40, 42, 47, 48, 56

Science & Society Picture Library   Pages 45, 46

Other illustrations were photographed from the original publications
by John Adams.

CONTENTS

FOREWORD

It has been a pleasure to assist in a very small way with the appearance of this imaginatively conceived, richly illustrated book. The compiler's very evident enthusiasm for his chosen theme shines through, bringing to life the typically optimistic and energetic attitudes the Victorians showed to the challenge of creating the world's first underground railway system.

Graphically portrayed here are the first decades of London's Underground, the part which London Transport used to call the 'subsurface lines' before it succumbed to the sloppy journalistic habit of dubbing the whole network 'the Tube', a term which is properly reserved for the later deep level lines.

The men who made the Metropolitan and Metropolitan District Railways were true pioneers, bravely facing and overcoming many challenges new and unfamiliar in the engineering knowledge and practice of their time. They had to decide how to ensure the safety of important buildings above and alongside their new railways by reducing the effects of vibration and settlement; how to estimate the lateral and vertical stresses of their tunnels; how best to divert gas, water and sewer service mains; how to design stations conducive to efficient passenger flow; and to find ways of maintaining road traffic during the works. Prominent in the solution of the problems faced was the great engineer Sir John Fowler (1817–98), who successfully organised this huge surgical operation on the circulatory organs of the metropolis. But no human is perfect; his attempt to design a fumeless steam locomotive was a total failure and the cleansing of the foul subterranean atmosphere had to await the arrival of electrification in the first years of the new century.

In remembering the engineers, we should never forget the army of labourers who toiled night and day with few mechanical aids in conditions well depicted here. After almost 150 years, the system these men built endures in modernised form, still serving London and, along with the tube lines, making the capital's life practicable by relieving what would otherwise be an impossible burden and congestion of motor traffic on the streets above.

Alan A. Jackson
Dorking, February 2000

INTRODUCTION

Certain books involve the reader in some effort – and this book]is one of them. With a little luck it may strain your imagination and stretch your mind. You are about to enter the world of the nineteenth century and if you try hard enough, this book will make the age of Queen Victoria and Sherlock Holmes come to life before your very eyes. Far-fetched? Perhaps, but not if you are prepared to suspend the reality of today and enter into the spirit of the period.

So you must unlearn your knowledge of the past 150 years and take on the mind-set and conventions of the mid-nineteenth century. Steam and the horse are the chief forms of motive power, whilst letters, telegrams and messenger boys are the means of communication. The only mass media are newspapers and magazines, few of which are illustrated, whilst photography is not long out of its infancy. The Great Exhibition of 1851 has opened the public's eyes to all manner of new wonders, chief among which are the miracles of engineering. Nothing is now impossible.

Of course, unless you put yourself in the mind of someone living in the period, a full appreciation of the subject will be difficult. For us, high-speed travel to Paris through the Channel Tunnel is a wonder of the age and we can watch it on television or home video. For the average Victorian, a solution to London's travel problems was equally momentous, at a time when only a few newspapers had illustrations of any kind and certainly not photographic ones.

The successful construction of the Metropolitan and Metropolitan District Railways was the wonder of the age we are concerned with here, an achievement to be regarded as remarkable as any marvel yet seen. We can be grateful for this – it means we can still find plenty of words and illustrations in contemporary books and newspapers. The euphoria did not last long, perhaps five or ten years at the most. As a result, later construction and even the completion of the Inner Circle aroused far less interest. And whilst that is entirely understandable, it does mean we have fewer illustrations and newspaper accounts of these events.

So join me now and put the twenty-first century out of your mind while you share the expectation, the anticipation, the speculation and the complete wonder of the construction of London's first underground railways.

Andrew Emmerson

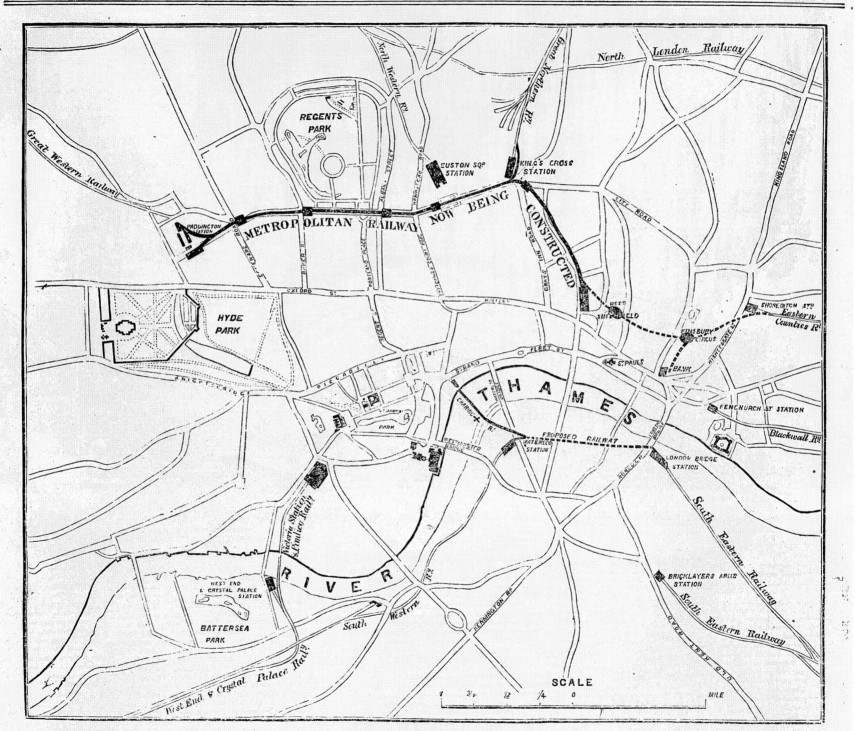

PLAN OF THE METROPOLITAN RAILWAY.

BEGINNINGS

Some enterprises reflect the accurate fulfilment of a single visionary's dream but most do not. The construction of London's first underground railway could almost be described as a plan that went wrong ... but set in motion something that achieved far more. That is because the original concept was of a Grand Central Terminus for all the trunk railways entering London; none of these reached the centre of the city and the construction of a single central station would have met a sorely felt need.

This, however, was not to be and 130 years later these termini are still spotted along the periphery of central London. What was achieved, a railway designed to provide connections between the main line stations and the City, was the genesis of the modern urban rapid transit system, arguably of much greater worth to a city which was as congested in 1860 as it is today.

This book is an album of pictures, not a chronicle, so historical discussion has been confined to putting our illustrations into context. But tribute must be paid to Sir Charles Pearson, City of London Solicitor since 1839, who had the vision of a city railway in humanitarian terms. His concept was a railway which would traverse with eight tracks the length of the Fleet Valley from King's Cross to Holborn Viaduct as part of an overall slum improvement scheme.

After some false starts a company was registered in 1853 as the North Metropolitan Railway; its scheme received Parliamentary approval the following year. The *Illustrated London News* reported that this interesting and novel undertaking would commence at the General Post Office in St Martin's-le-Grand and proceed beneath the streets and roads of the metropolis all the way to the terminus of the Great Western Railway at Paddington, a distance of four and a half miles.

Needless to say, public reaction was not entirely favourable. Hosts of objections were raised and all manner of evils prophesied. Learned engineers were not wanting to foretell how the projected tunnel must fall in from the mere weight of the traffic in the streets above, and how the adjacent houses would not only be shaken to their foundations by the vibration caused by the engines, but the families residing in them would be one and all poisoned by the sulphurous exhalations from the fuel with which the boilers were heated.

All the same, the North Metropolitan Railway was a dream which did indeed become reality; many other visions conceived at the same time sadly did not. Grand schemes for uniting London's main line railways and plans for relieving traffic congestion in the Metropolis were legion at this time.

Opposite One of the first maps published of the original route of the Metropolitan Railway, at a time when it was still under construction. An eastward extension was already planned and is shown with a pecked line. At this stage its route was conjectural, however. (*Illustrated London News*, 7th April 1860)

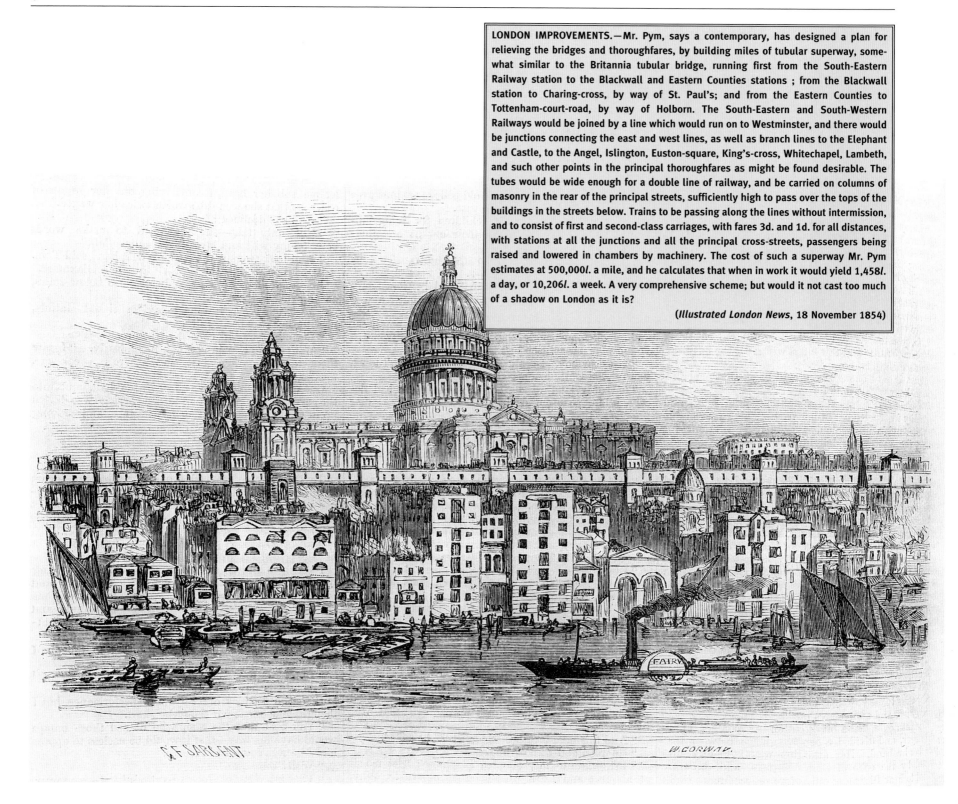

LONDON IMPROVEMENTS.—Mr. Pym, says a contemporary, has designed a plan for relieving the bridges and thoroughfares, by building miles of tubular superway, somewhat similar to the Britannia tubular bridge, running first from the South-Eastern Railway station to the Blackwall and Eastern Counties stations ; from the Blackwall station to Charing-cross, by way of St. Paul's; and from the Eastern Counties to Tottenham-court-road, by way of Holborn. The South-Eastern and South-Western Railways would be joined by a line which would run on to Westminster, and there would be junctions connecting the east and west lines, as well as branch lines to the Elephant and Castle, to the Angel, Islington, Euston-square, King's-cross, Whitechapel, Lambeth, and such other points in the principal thoroughfares as might be found desirable. The tubes would be wide enough for a double line of railway, and be carried on columns of masonry in the rear of the principal streets, sufficiently high to pass over the tops of the buildings in the streets below. Trains to be passing along the lines without intermission, and to consist of first and second-class carriages, with fares 3d. and 1d. for all distances, with stations at all the junctions and all the principal cross-streets, passengers being raised and lowered in chambers by machinery. The cost of such a superway Mr. Pym estimates at 500,000*l.* a mile, and he calculates that when in work it would yield 1,458*l.* a day, or 10,206*l.* a week. A very comprehensive scheme; but would it not cast too much of a shadow on London as it is?

(*Illustrated London News*, 18 November 1854)

MIGHT-HAVE-BEENS

Underground railways running in tunnels were only one idea among several solutions proposed to London's traffic problems in the mid-nineteenth century. Two schemes deliberated by the Select Committee on Metropolitan Communications in 1855 were Sir Joseph Paxton's Grand Girdle Railway and Boulevard Under Glass together with William Moseley's Crystal Way. Also known as the Grand Victorian Way, the former envisaged a covered way linking each of the trunk railways and encircling the metropolis; it was to be ten miles long in the form of a large arcade of glass and iron, 72 feet wide and 102 feet high. Eight railway tracks would be provided, four for express trains and four local.

The Crystal Way was to be a slightly more modest affair, formed of a continuous arcaded shopping passage with a twin track railway below. The structure would have been thirty feet wide and seventy-eight feet tall. As with Paxton's scheme the trains would have employed atmospheric power.

John Pym's scheme of November 1854 offered the alternative solution of a railway entirely above the city streets. Paradoxically, if carried out, this would also have been London's first tube railway, since it envisaged iron tubes carried on pillars of masonry. The tubes, intended to carry a double line of railway, were to be lighted by ornamental windows on each side and by gas at night and also warmed and ventilated during the different seasons of the year.

The Super-way was the name given to his tubular scheme. Similar in construction to Stephenson's Britannia Tubular Bridge, it was to run from the South Eastern Railway at London Bridge to the Blackwall and Eastern Counties Railway at Fenchurch Street; from the Blackwall station to Charing Cross by way of St Paul's and from the Eastern Counties to Tottenham Court Road by way of Holborn. The South Eastern and London & South Western Railways would be joined by a line which would run on to Westminster, and there would be junctions connecting the East and West lines, as well as branch lines to the Elephant and Castle, to the Angel, Islington, Euston Square, King's Cross, Whitechapel, Lambeth, and such other points in the principal thoroughfares as might be found desirable. The tubes would be wide enough for a double line of railway, and be carried on columns of masonry in the rear of principal streets, sufficiently high to pass over the tops of the buildings in the streets below. According to a contemporary account, 'trains will pass along the lines without intermission, and consist of First- and Second-class carriages, with fares of 3d and 1d for all distances, with stations at all principal cross-streets, passengers being raised and lowered in chambers by machinery'.

Pym's Super-Way as it would have appeared from the Thames, passing in front of St Paul's Cathedral. (Illustration from *London Journal*, 1861)

The Crystal Way – with an appearance inspired no doubt by Joseph Paxton's 1851 Crystal Palace – was an elaborate plan of 1854 for a railway at subsurface level surmounted by what looks rather like a modern covered shopping centre. It was designed by William Moseley, whose other work included lunatic asylums. It was envisaged to run from Cheapside to Oxford Circus with a branch to Piccadilly, and around 400 buildings would have needed to be demolished to make the railway possible. This, coupled with his ill-worked-out methods of atmospheric propulsion and train operation, doomed the idea to failure before it left the drawing board.

Right A sectional view of the 'London Railway' (1841), a proposed overhead system with a route similar to the Circle Line in its intention to link London's newly completed main line termini. The cross sections of the track show the pneumatic tube that would have propelled the trains. The casually seated figures at the ends of the trains are presumably guards or conductors. The railway's undesirable visual impact on the centre of London, and the plan for it to occupy Southwark and Waterloo bridges in order to serve Waterloo station, made it unacceptable to the authorities.

To have a railway, after the American fashion, passing through a densely-populous district, and crossing on the level our overcrowded streets and thoroughfares, was utterly out of the question; and scarcely less so to carry an unsightly viaduct through the heart of the metropolis. The only alternative was that adopted by the Metropolitan Company—namely, that of an underground communication, by which the most densely-crowded districts could be traversed without the slightest annoyance or obstruction to the existing traffic.
(*Illustrated London News*, 7th April 1860)

PROMISE …

The following extracts from documents published in 1861 and quoted both in Pinks's 'History of Clerkenwell' and the *London Journal* (June 1862) will give some notion of what was intended. One wonders whether the people who drafted these words really believed their own hyperbole or whether this was a cynical attempt to hoodwink a gullible public.

The railway from the Great Western to the Post-office will be a double line of mixed gauge, adapted for carriages on both the narrow and broad gauges, with two additional lines of rails on the narrow gauge from the Great Northern Railway to the City, for the accommodation of short trains on that line, and to meet the requirements of the dead meat market in Copenhagen-fields when the contemplated arrangements with the Great Northern Railway Company and the Corporation of London are satisfactorily concluded. The arcade through which the railway will be carried will be spacious, dry, well lighted, and ventilated, and, by the mode of working the trains, entirely free of smoke and steam.

The trains will be approached by wide and easy stairs, not involving more than the ordinary descent from the drawing-room to the dining-room. The carriages will be spacious, and adapted for the London traffic; they will be fitted up with every comfort, and mirrors and lights will altogether exclude the idea of under-ground travelling. The trains will be propelled by locomotive engines moved by steam generated from heated water carried with the engines, with an apparatus for condensing the waste steam, by which means all annoyance from smoke, grit, and steam will be avoided.

The trains will be run in regular succession, at intervals of five minutes, with additional trains during the busy hours of the morning and afternoon. From their frequency they will be light and of nearly uniform weight; the passengers to take up and set down at each station, from the shortness of the interval between one train and another, will be few; fifteen are taken as the average, and will require but a momentary stoppage. The gradients will be uniformly good, and the rails will not be liable to be rendered slippery and dirty by the weather or other external influences. The trains will therefore be worked with a clock-work regularity, which is all-important for the business traffic of the metropolis, and will more than compensate for the comparatively low speed which will be attained – fifteen miles per hour, including stoppages, is reckoned on.

As the railway and carriages will always be under cover, they will not be liable to damage from the weather, and will, in other respects, be more economically managed and maintained. It is impossible to conceive a system of railway communication better adapted for the accommodation of the London passenger traffic.

One of the novelties is the lighting of the carriages, which is not like that which is usually adopted in the railways, but rather like that to be found in a drawing-room. In each compartment there are at least two lights of compressed gas, producing such a brilliant light as to enable a passenger to read even the smallest print with the greatest ease. Another and still greater novelty is the locomotive, which has been specially devised for the working of the line. This engine, which has been built by the firm of Stephenson, at Newcastle, has this peculiarity, that it runs for a given time – two miles and a half – without sending forth steam, which it condenses, and without causing smoke, which it consumes.

… AND REALITY

The reality, available to the public between Paddington and Farringdon Street from 10th January 1863, was rather different, as people soon found out and as Pinks made plain.

For weeks [after opening] the stations were thronged with people desirous of riding, and the traffic was comparatively nothing to what it might have been if the Great Western Company had carried over the rails all who desired to ride; but the accommodation was somewhat scanty, and the dwellers out of town, who desired a quick ride to and from the City, found that they could not depend upon the railway. The consequence was that the number of riders fell off, and other causes besides the uncertainly of obtaining trains also operated injuriously to the traffic. The public has been promised to be carried in handsome and well-lighted carriages through a tunnel free from smell; but very shortly after the line was opened, old dingy carriages, lighted with oil, were no rarity, and, worse, than all, the tunnel was far from being free of sulphuric fumes, and of blended smells from coke and steam.

So low did the traffic become, and from nothing but these causes, that instead of clearing £600 a day, as was reasonably estimated in 1856, the traffic returns for a whole week were only £1885 (with Sunday traffic), scarcely half that which had been estimated. Matters were not at all smoothed by a quarrel which now occurred between the two companies, the Great Western as lessees, and the Metropolitan as proprietors. The former company desired some modification of the terms upon which they worked the line. The latter refused to accede to the request, and then the Great Western Company's Directors, on the 18th July, 1863, notified that they would not work the line after the 30th September. The Metropolitan Company took the responsibilities thus thrown upon them, and made arrangements for continuing the traffic on the 1st of October. The Directors of the Great Western, seemingly desirous of compelling the Metropolitan Company to accede to their terms, published in the August time-table a notification that they would not be responsible for the traffic after the last train on the 10th of that month, thus throwing the Metropolitan Company on their own resources. Within a few days, with the assistance of the Great Northern Company, the Directors of the Metropolitan Company were enabled to make an endeavour to meet their extraordinary position, and they issued a notice to the public detailing the circumstances by which they were surrounded. The notice concluded as follows: 'The Metropolitan Directors are not unmindful of the responsibilities of their position, but they are confident that the Metropolitan line will ere long be worked in a manner and to the extent that was originally intended, which it has not hitherto been, nor, as events have made apparent, was ever likely to be whilst in the hands of the Great Western Company, and whereby alone it can secure its fair share of the enormous local traffic requiring accommodation. It will be the object of the Metropolitan Directors to bring into action such a system of working, so soon as they can obtain the requisite stock, whereby they feel assured that the convenience of the public will be much enhanced, and the receipts of the company greatly increased. The Directors are making all necessary arrangements, and in the meantime have only to ask from the public every reasonable indulgence, and from the shareholders their full confidence.'

PROPOSED STATION AT BAKER STREET.

BAKER STREET

This engraving conveys a very fair impression of the Baker Street Station as built; the platforms will be recognisable to today's passengers.
(Illustration from *Illustrated London News*, 7th April 1860)

The railway will have a clear width of 28 feet 6 inches, and will consist of a double line of both broad and narrow gauge. The rails are to rest on gravel ballast, which system effectually prevents all vibration to adjoining property.

An elliptical arch of beautiful outline, formed of six 4½ inch rings of brickwork, set in hydraulic lime and Portland cement where required, will protect the tunnelled portion of the way, and there will be two distinct junctions at the western end, one leading to the Great Western hotel, and the other to the main line. The arched bell-mouths (as they are technically termed) of these junctions will be constructed of wrought-iron. There will also be a junction formed at the Great Northern railway, King's-cross, in connexion with the City.

In addition to the frequent openings that this peculiar railway will have to the atmosphere, the trains themselves are to be ventilated by an ingenious contrivance of the engineer by which the deleterious gases of combustion are not generated. The carriages also will be as light as any drawing-room.

Building News, 2nd November 1860.

CONSTRUCTION BEGINS

It is almost impossible to over-estimate the disruption and confusion caused by the construction of the Metropolitan Railway and fortunately the Victorian writers were well equipped to put this into words.

Perhaps the most noteworthy of all tunnels is the Metropolitan or Underground Railway. When it was first proposed, the idea of a railway for human beings to travel along under the streets and among the sewers was regarded with amusement if not contempt. The omnibus and cab interests, as represented by their drivers, forgetting what their predecessors the stage coachmen had done under similar circumstances, were eminently facetious on the various aspects of the subject, and many jokes, good and bad, were made thereon.

Railway work in the open has difficulties enough, but the bed of a London thoroughfare has been compared to the human body – full of veins and arteries which it is death to cut. No sooner is the ground opened than these channels of gas and water, of sewers and telegraphs are seen 'as close together as the pipes of a church organ'. The engineers of the Metropolitan Railway had, to begin with, to remove these old channels to the sides of the roadway, and then to cut their way between, 'with the delicacy of a surgical operation' . . .

The work of constructing this remarkable railway eventually became, as it must be allowed, somewhat wearisome to the inhabitants of the New Road. A few wooden houses on wheels first made their appearance, and planted themselves by the gutter; then came some wagons loaded with timber, and accompanied by sundry gravel-coloured men with picks and shovels. A day or two afterwards, a few hundred yards of roadway were enclosed, the ordinary traffic being, of course, driven into the side streets; then followed troops of navvies, horses, and engines arrived, who soon disappeared within the enclosure and down the shafts. The exact operations could be but dimly seen or heard from the street by the curious observer who gazed between the tall boards that shut him out; but paterfamilias, from his house hard by, could look down on an infinite chaos of timber, shaft holes, ascending and descending chains and iron buckets which brought rubbish from below to be carted away; or perhaps one morning he found workmen had been kindly shoring up his family abode with huge timbers to make it safer. 'A wet week comes, and the gravel in his front garden turns to clay; the tradespeople tread it backwards and forwards to and from the street door; he can hardly get out to business or home to supper without slipping, and he strongly objects to a temporary way of wet planks, erected for his use and the use of the passers-by, over a yawning cavern underneath the pavement.'

(F.S. Williams: 'Our Iron Roads', 5th edition, London: Bemrose & Son, 1884)

Note that during this period two major streets changed their names: Victoria Street to Farringdon Road and New Road to Euston Road. In addition Coppice Row is now known as Ray Street. No alteration has been made to period documents quoted here, nor to the original spelling and punctuation.

DIGGING THE TRENCH FOR A TUNNEL

This is the first of two highly atmospheric illustrations taken from a French survey of scientific marvels. Although the views do not represent any identifiable locality, they were nonetheless commissioned specially for this book and can be considered reasonably accurate and representative.

This drawing clearly shows the method of construction. The first cuttings have been dug and the retaining walls are being built.
(Illustration from Figuier: 'Les Nouvelles Conquêtes de la Science', vol. 2)

TRANSFORMING THE CUTTING INTO A TUNNEL

Here a roof of iron girders is being placed across the cutting where a street crosses – note the property which has been demolished and how the billposters have wasted no time in using this opportunity.
(Illustration from Figuier: 'Les Nouvelles Conquêtes de la Science', vol. 2)

THE ENGRAVING PROCESS

Most of the illustrations in this book are derived from woodcuts; a few are reproductions of lithographs (printed with a stone block), steel engravings or electrotypes (described below). In our period the woodcut reigned supreme and although a few photographs also exist, they were not yet a medium seen in books or newspapers. Photography was in fact a new art and a relatively expensive one, and although John Fowler had photographs taken of the construction of the Metropolitan Railway, the expense and technology of the process meant that photographs could not be reproduced cheaply. To most people of the time photography was in fact an expensive high-tech novelty.

Daily newspapers did not contain pictures in those days and when these appeared in new publications such the *Illustrated London News* and its now forgotten rival, the *Illustrated Times*, the success of these newcomers was assured. Readers were desperate to see the events described and the publishers had to oblige them. To do this the illustrations had to be produced with appropriate technology and that technology was the hand-drawn woodcut.

In this technique, illustrations were engraved on blocks of wood having a fine, hard texture; generally boxwood was used. The drawings were made by artists who sketched the scene by day and drew a fair copy of the illustrations by night. It was thankless work, probably forgotten within a fortnight, and probably poorly paid. This was only part of the process, since these drawings had then to be copied, in reverse of course, onto the wood blocks by skilled engravers.

Artist and engraver each made his own contribution and the sole criticism that can be levelled at these workers is that occasionally the artist misunderstood some technicality or the engraver formed a letter of the alphabet backwards. The intricacies of locomotive valve-gear or of points and crossings in railway track occasionally defeated the sketchers, whilst back-to-front 'S's are often seen (but should be overlooked as an amusing curiosity). Examples of these 'errors' can be found in this book, and considering the speed with which these illustrations were prepared (and required) it is remarkable that more mistakes were not created.

As technology matured towards the end of the nineteenth century the wood block was replaced by the 'electrotype' or 'zincograph', a zinc printing plate made electrochemically by a photo-graphic process (and afterwards this process was developed further to enable photographs to be reproduced in the half-tone process).

THE METROPOLITAN RAILWAY-MACHINE FOR HOISTING UP THE EARTH FROM BELOW.—SKETCHED IN THE EUSTON-ROAD

VIEW OF THE TUNNEL OF THE METROPOLITAN RAILWAY, SHOWING THE WORKS IN PROGRESS

DIGGING UP THE EUSTON ROAD

Machine for hoisting earth, sketched in the Euston Road ran the caption, and no doubt to the Victorian onlooker it was as monstrous as one of the giant tunnelling machines which cut the Channel Tunnel would be to the modern observer.

(Illustration from *Illustrated Times*, 19th October 1861)

Work in the tunnel below is depicted in the second illustration.

KING'S CROSS

Work next to the Euston Road at King's Cross with plenty of activity. This is the 'cover' operation of the cut and cover system and a brick arch is being built over the cutting. Note the contractor's extensive temporary railway system.

(Illustration from *London Journal*, November 1861)

THE LONG DAY

The workman's day was a long one and, during winter, braziers had to be lit at the start and end of the working day. Today's health and safety officers would doubtless have plenty to say about the working practices seen in this illustration from an unknown source.

CONSTRUCTING THE TUNNELS

Wooden shoring retains the excavated areas as brickwork is put in. The massive amount of timber required and the extensive use of manual labour on a 24-hour basis are apparent.

CROSS SECTION OF THE EUSTON ROAD
(*Facing page*)

This engineer's drawing shows the extent of shoring up necessary where the Tottenham Court Road crosses the Euston Road (then called the New Road) and becomes Hampstead Road. Temporary tracks (not broad gauge) have been sketched in. It also illustrates the shoring up of buildings against the effects of excavation.

TOTTENHAM COURT ROAD

HAMPSTEAD ROAD

J. NEWTON. 136

DIETMAN

SMITH & KNIGHT, CONT

LEVEL OF PERMANENT WAY

JOHN FOWLER Esq. Eng.

THE WORKS FOR THE UNDERGROUND RAILWAY AT COPPICE-ROW, CLERKENWELL.

CUT AND COVER AT KING'S CROSS

The destruction of property was significant, as seen in this view from the east of King's Cross main line station (which is seen on the right).

(Illustration from *Illustrated London News*, 2nd February 1861)

CHAOS AT STREET LEVEL – Coppice Row (today named Ray Street) *(Facing page)*

The frenzied activity of the advertising bill stickers compares with that of today's grafitti-scrawlers This illustration also demonstrates the very elaborate shoring-up required for buildings with minimal foundations once excavation began. William J. Pinks, paraphrasing Hollingshead's 'Underground London', described the chaos caused by closing off streets for trenching:

> At the time the excavation was going on in Coppice-row, the thoroughfares were in a most deplorable state. The roadway from Wharton-street to the corner of Exmouth-street was completely shut up from the public, and a high hoarding prevented all inspection of the works which were going on. The same was the case with the roadway from Exmouth-street to beyond Bowling-green-lane. The footways along these thoroughfares, though open to passengers, were in a most inconvenient state for traffic, for 'struts' were placed up to most of the houses to keep them from falling in, and the pavement in many places was sunken, making the path dangerously uneven. Nor were these all the troubles, for through the whole line where the tunnel came near to buildings those buildings gave every indication of speedy dissolution, and many houses, having been reported by the police surveyor as unsafe, were vacated by their occupants. (Pinks, 'History of Clerkenwell')

(Illustration from *Illustrated Times*, 18th January 1862)

THE FLEET DITCH AT PEACE

Today it is hard to envisage Clerkenwell as a pastoral neighbourhood but its once-rural nature is still recalled by street names such as Saffron Hill, Field Lane, Lily, Turnmill and Vine Streets. In this spirit the *Illustrated London News*'s writer began to wax lyrical:

Our view was sketched at the foot of Frederick-street, Gray's-inn-road, at its junction with Bagnigge-wells-road, formerly celebrated, among other things, for its spa and for containing the summer residence of Nell Gwynne. Looking towards King's-cross, the streets seen in our Engraving through which the Metropolitan Railroad has breached its way are – first, in the distance, Britannia-street, next Swinton-street, then Acton-street and finally Frederick-street. It is at this point that the Fleet Ditch is temporarily diverted from its course, previously to its being boxed up, as it is at King's-cross, in an iron tube, now a sewer, but once a crystal stream running its short but pleasant career from smiling uplands through orchards, gardens and meadows, to slide at last, 'babbling o' green fields', into what was then the 'silver Thames'.

(*Illustrated London News*, 15th February 1862)

Further explanation is found in Fry's 'London Guide' [London: W.H. Allen & Co., 1894] which stated: 'Bagnigge Wells Road, near King's Cross, was once noted for its mineral spring, and for tea gardens, opened to the public in 1758 and finally closed in June 1841.' Bagnigge Wells Road is today named King's Cross Road.

THE FLEET SEWER BURSTS

Within five months of the date of the previous scene, the Fleet had burst its bounds in a most dramatic way, such that it would delay the opening of the new railway by several months.

On the night of Sunday, June 15th 1862 a sinking of the earth was observed on the west side of the new street, at a very short distance from the curve of the street which leads to Warner-street. This was followed by a rush of sewer water into adjacent cellars. The cause was soon discovered to be from the breaking in of the crown of the arch to the Fleet Sewer – the Black River of North London. Immediate steps were taken by the officers of the railway contractors to prevent their works becoming submerged, and their efforts were seconded by the officers of the Metropolitan Board of Works, the sewers being vested in the hands of that body. The hours of Monday, Monday night, Tuesday, Tuesday night, and part of Wednesday were spent in this endeavour. On Wednesday afternoon the breakage was becoming worse. The pavement was found to be sinking still further, and it needed but little knowledge for one to be aware that if the roadway sank on the sewer and stopped its passage the stream of many thousands gallons a minute would find a vent somewhere, and that vent would be most likely the scarcely completed works of the railway. Mighty dams had been placed against the masonry-like walls of the railway to give them additional strength; but at about four o'clock the earth around the spot of the breakage was felt to shake, as if under the influence of an earthquake. Then there was a cry of alarm, and men were to be seen hurrying from the point with all speed. The next few moments were moments of terror and horror. Suddenly the network of scaffolding, composed of the largest and heaviest beams it was possible to obtain, was hurled in the air, and fell to the earth with a crash like thunder, amid the screams and shouts of thousands of spectators, whose excited fancies pictured some helpless workmen in the ruins. There was an intense silence for a moment, and then the immense piers of brickwork, about fifty or sixty feet in height, were to be seen slowly moving from the bottom. The next phase was watched for with breathless anxiety and soon came. There was a gravel path at the bottom of the excavation near the feet of the piers, and this was to be seen, as though an indissoluble mass, slowly moving on one side, and then the dark foetid liquid covered all, and rolled its way towards the mouth of the tunnel, tearing down, as it went, all obstructions, and snapping like straws the strongest piles of massive timber. The writer was an eye-witness of the whole scene, and at this moment stood at the mouth of the tunnel, by the side of the manager of the works and the engineers, all of whom had been busily striving to prevent this crowning calamity.

No time was spent in useless regrets; the contractors of the company exerted themselves to provide a channel for the water to run off into the Thames, which was done through an old drain, and the officers of the Metropolitan Board of Works worked very hard to make a temporary channel, which, after many difficulties had been overcome, was executed; the old sewer was meanwhile rebuilt, and the injury to the railway was solidly repaired. (Pinks, 'History of Clerkenwell')

The illustration shows a broad panorama of the destruction. (*Illustrated London News*, 28th June 1862, op cit.)

KING'S CROSS JUNCTIONS

Immediately west of the original King's Cross station of the Metropolitan Railway (King's Cross Thameslink occupies the site today) were some complex junctions with the Great Northern Railway in tunnel. Subsequent construction of the City Widened Lines with links to the Midland Railway and the start of a tunnel towards the LNWR at Euston (never completed) made the whole area extremely complicated.

These works at King's Cross were noted by John Hollingshead in 'Underground London' (Groombridge & Co., 1862) as the 'important centre of the Metropolitan Railway works' and where 'the chief engineering difficulties of the work have arisen'. *The Builder* (19th January 1861) described it as 'a work of no common difficulty, a work calculated to keep awake all who are concerned in it'. The layout of this underground junction inspired several writers to describe it in some detail. Here is the original description for this illustration:

This view shows the double bell-mouth and groining at King's-cross, which are formed to allow the junction of two branch lines by which this railway is connected with the Great Northern Railway. The whole of this bell-mouth is executed in brickwork, the greatest span being about 45 feet.

The road on the left shows the line to the east side of the Great Northern, and is completed.

The two branch lines, passing as they will do on each side of the Great Northern station, will enable trains to work continuously from stations on the Great Northern to the City without interruption, and without crossing any of the main lines of rail; thus practically extending that railway to the City, and by the authorised London, Chatham and Dover Railway &c., to Brighton and the Continent. The main line, seen on the right, is being carried forward to Victoria-street and Smithfield.

The earth ... being removed ... is shot down into waggons, taken by temporary rails to the Great Northern and so to Wood-green. About 500 yards of stuff are taken out every day. At the other end of the line the excavated material is taken away, in a similar manner to that just now described, to Brentford, to form an embankment there. Much of the gravel is used in the works for concrete and as ballast.

(*The Builder*, 19th January 1861)

FOWLER'S GHOST AT PRAED STREET JUNCTION

This view dates from early 1862 and shows the bell-mouth junction between Edgware Road and Paddington stations known as Praed Street Junction. Bro. Bill, the artist, seems to have been defeated in his representation of the dual-gauge trackwork but we can forgive him as he has provided us with a rare and valuable view of *Fowler's Ghost*, a locomotive otherwise seen only in two photographs. For all the deficiencies of the drawing, to find another illustration is most gratifying. The article accompanying this illustration had this to say of the locomotive:

> The greatest difficulty of all the many that had to be overcome [in constructing the railway] consisted in constructing an engine such as that represented in our engraving, which should be at once of great power and speed, capable of consuming its own smoke, and, above all, giving off no steam. To meet these requirements, Mr Fowler has constructed an engine which, in the open air, works like a common locomotive. In the tunnel it consumes its own smoke, or rather makes none, and by condensing its own steam, gives off not a particle of vapour.

The locomotive was not in fact the success that this report suggested and disappeared soon afterwards. In this view, it is seen hauling some freight down from the GWR at Bishops Road – note the typical guard's seat perched atop the roof of the van. Note also the glimmer of the gas jets under the roof and at the intersection of the arches – the Metropolitan Railway was initially very concerned that passengers should not be upset by the darkness below ground. 'Gas will supply the place of the sun' was the company's proud boast and the *Illustrated London News* of 15th February 1862 confirmed that 'the whole route [in tunnel] is well lighted with gas'.

The Metropolitan Railway went out of its way to maintain public interest during its construction, achieving this by affording facilities to the press to make illustrations such as this and generally ingratiating itself with reporters. The writer of the articles which originally accompanied this illustration must have been extremely impressed (or treated to an excellent lunch), for he wrote:

> Although this curious and unique metropolitan railway has been termed underground, or subterranean, for nearly half its length it is open to the light and air of heaven, and where it does pass for various lengths beneath the surface, it is so well lighted and ventilated that the tunnels, instead of being close, dark, damp and offensive are wide, spacious, clean and luminous, and more like a well-kept street at night, than a subterranean passage through the very heart of the metropolis.

(Illustration from *London Journal*, January 1862, p. 24)

THE LINE OPENS

The rupture of the Fleet sewer and technical delays concerning signalling were among problems which contrived to delay the intended 1862 opening but eventually, on 10th January 1863, the Metropolitan Railway between Paddington (Bishops Road) and Farringdon Road was finally opened to the public, following a ceremonial banquet the day before. Regrettably, the architect of the whole scheme, Charles Pearson, never saw this day, having died the previous September. All the same, the railway fulfilled his expectations and notwithstanding a temporary falling off in traffic soon after opening, became a notable success. At times passengers had to wait for the departure of three or four trains before they could board, and plans were soon made for extending the line, first to Moorgate Street and High Street (Kensington) and later, with the collaboration of the Metropolitan District Railway, completing the whole of the Inner Circle railway.

Opening trip

At length, towards the end of 1862, it was definitely announced that the line would open early in the new year. The temporary station in Farringdon-road was fitted up in its whole length (about nine hundred feet) as a dining hall, and tables were arranged for about seven hundred guests. On the 9th of January a very large company, composed of members of the two Houses of Parliament, representatives of the Press, well-known engineers, the highest members of the City Corporation, and most of the local gentry, assembled at the Great Western Station, at Paddington. The company first viewed the Bishop's-road Station, and then started, in the first *bona fide* passenger train ever run, amid loud and enthusiastic cheers from people who crowded the unfinished walls. At each station between Paddington and Clerkenwell – viz., Edgware-road, Baker-street, Portland-road, Gower-street, and King's-cross the passengers alighted and made an inspection, and the greatest delight was expressed at all that was to be seen, and at the great comfort with which the journey was made. The air was very clear, the carriages exceedingly comfortable – all well lighted with gas, cushioned, and carpeted – and everything that could be wished. When the train ran into Farringdon-road Station the visitors were welcomed with every demonstration of joy. Bands of music were playing, flags waving, people cheering, and such like, and then the visitors were ushered into the temporary but handsomely fitted dining hall, in which was spread a most sumptuous banquet. In the speeches made after the banquet full justice was done to the patience and perseverance which had overcome all the difficulties besetting the work, and no small tribute was paid to the genius of Charles Pearson, then lately deceased, in whose mind the idea of the railway first arose, and who certainly did no little towards the carrying out of the great undertaking. The next morning the first public trains ran, and a great rush of people to ride by the new road testified to the pent-up curiosity of the general public. (Pinks, op. cit.)

The main trunk line, station, and sidings of the Underground Metropolitan Railway were officially inspected on Saturday morning last by the Government Inspector of Railways, appointed by the Board of Trade. The engineers of the Metropolitan Railway, assisted by the engineers of the various lines terminating in the metropolis, and several civil engineers, the chairman, deputy-chairman, directory, secretary, and other officers belonging to the railway company, accompanied the inspector. After a minute survey of the line, the rails, points, sidings, bridges, and the new brickwork in the vicinity of the late accident, which gave general satisfaction, the party proceeded in carriages propelled by one of the company's locomotive engines along the line at various rates of speed, stopping at the several stations, and shunting on the sidings, in order to test the efficiency of the apparatus and its appliances. In the afternoon two or three hundred gentlemen—shareholders and others—were conveyed along the line from the Victoria station to the terminus in a train of carriages and trucks drawn by two engines. The train stopped at all the stations, to give an opportunity of observation; and on the return journey refreshments were provided at the Edgware-road station. The general feeling was evidently that of agreeable disappointment—the open cutting being more extensive, and the tunnels better lighted and ventilated, than was expected. The journey was performed in carriages belonging to the Great Western Company, by whom, we understand, the line is to be worked. The construction of this railway is now so far advanced as to render it pretty certain that the line will be open to the public early in October.

The Victoria Station mentioned in this press report (*London Journal*, September 1862) was opened as Farringdon Street. The 'late accident' referred to is probably the bursting of the Fleet sewer.

The inspection train made up with broad gauge GWR coaches and
belonging to the contractor, Smith & Knight, enters Portland Road Station
(now Great Portland Street) to the roar of hurrahs on 30th August 1862.
(*Illustrated London News*, 13th September 1862)

This vast (250ft by 50ft) tent lined with red and white cloth was erected inside the temporary terminus at Farringdon Street for the ceremonial dinner, attended by about 700 guests, on 9th January 1863.

(*Illustrated London News*, 17th January 1863)

The Metropolitan Railway was fairly opened to the public on the 10th inst., and it was calculated that more than 30,000 persons were carried over the line in the course of the day. Indeed, the desire to travel by this line on the opening day was more than the directors had provided for; and from nine o'clock in the morning till past mid-day it was impossible to obtain a place in the up or Cityward line at any of the mid stations. In the evening the tide turned, and the crush at the Farringdon-street station was as great as at the doors of a theatre on the first night of some popular performer. Some lightening of the pressure was obtained by the Great Western lending some of their engines and carriages supplemental to the rolling stock of the company. Notwithstanding the throng, it is gratifying to add that no accident occurred, and the report of the passengers was unanimous in favour of the smoothness and comfort of the line.

(*Illustrated London News*, 17th January 1863)

The illustration shows the first public train at Bishop's Road (Paddington) station on 10th January 1863. The assorted coaching stock is broad gauge, provided by the Great Western Railway, which worked trains initially for the Metropolitan. The passengers are predominantly workmen and artisans; it is likely that top-hatted men are railway police.

(Illustration from *Illustrated Times*, 17th January 1863)

BAKER STREET, 1863

In many ways similar to Gower Street station, the entrances to the original station here were on either side of the Marylebone Road, broad flights of stairs leading down to the platforms. This part of the station was immediately underneath the roadway. Great ingenuity was observed in the construction of the station, for although deep underground, it enjoyed the advantage of daylight, which was made to glance down from the roadway above through long shafts lined with white glazed tiles. Today these shafts have been covered over and illuminated artificially. This handsome 1863 view is not an engraving but a chromolithograph by Samuel J. Hodson. It is interesting to compare it with the picture on page 13.

DORÉ: THE WORKMEN'S TRAIN

This and other drawings of 1870s London scenes ('London, A Pilgrimage', 1871) by the great French illustrator Gustave Doré (1823–83) are notable more for their overall effect than the attention to minute detail. And so in this particular picture – entitled *Workmen's train, early morning* and probably of Baker Street or Gower Street (now Euston Square), the artist fails to capture the correct shape of the curved roof (cf. opposite and page 35) or the lines of the rolling stock. We can overlook this and note the other authentic details such as the sign directing third class passengers where to wait. The Metropolitan was the first London railway to operate workmen's cheap fare trains, introducing them in May 1864 ahead of any statutory requirement. Initially there were two trains each way starting at 5.30am and 5.40am; return was allowed by any train on the same day. By 1883 twelve such trains were operating daily, starting between 5.13am and 6.19am.

PORTLAND ROAD (now Great Portland Street) as built, 1863

This sectional view is taken from an unknown German publication but it is certainly remarkable for the amount of detail incorporated. The 4-4-OT locomotive and the rigid eight-wheeler Metropolitan carriages are correctly shown along with the platform arrangements. The nameboards claim the station serves 'Regent's Park East and Zoological Gardens', but the entrance to the latter is almost a mile away. The domed surface structures lasted only nine years.

Portland-road station is the next one [after Gower-street]. It is above ground, and occupies the site of the once verdant oval inclosure near Trinity Church. One booking-office here suffices; and the lighting and ventilation are effected by a pair of domes, and by openings in the crown of the arch. The communication with the platforms is by stairs and galleries across the line, which, sustained by trelliswork, have a light and pleasing effect. (Pinks, op. cit.)

GOWER STREET (now Euston Square)

For some reason this station is one of the best described of all the stations on the Inner Circle, probably on account of its remarkable lighting system, which it shared with Baker Street station.

Passing under the New-road, the next station is at Gower-street. The platforms here are under the footpaths of the road and with the railway are spanned by a huge arch of forty-five feet opening. The sides of the arch are perforated with openings at intervals of ten feet; these openings are continued into the forecourts or gardens of the houses where they emerge, and are covered with glass, the whole having the appearance of windows, with elongated reveals, lined with glazed white earthenware tiles. Thus both direct and reflected rays of light impinge upon each platform, and completely light the whole substructure. Ingress and egress to the station are effected by means of booking offices on the north and south sides of the Euston-road, in the gardens of the houses, and by wide exit and entrance stairs, leading from the booking offices to the platforms. This station, with its numerous intersected and intersecting arches, is novel in its appearance and imposing in its effects. (Pinks, op. cit.)

Of the stations the majority have roofs of the ordinary kind, open to the sky; but two of them, namely, Baker Street and Gower Street, are completely underground stations, and their roofs are formed by the arches of brickwork immediately below the streets. The openings are entirely lined with white glazed tiles, and the outward ends open into an area, the back of which is inclined at an angle of 45 degrees, and the whole also lined with white glazed tiles, and covered with glass, except where some iron gratings are provided for ventilation. The tiles reflect the daylight so powerfully that but little gas is required for the illumination of the station in the day-time. ('Routledge's Guide to London'; London: George Routledge & Sons, 1885)

JUNCTION OF THE GREAT NORTHERN, MIDLAND, AND METROPOLITAN RAILWAYS AT KING'S-CROSS.

KING'S CROSS, west end of station

Growth in traffic made it necessary to build an additional pair of tracks between King's Cross and Farringdon Street; this work was completed on 17th February 1868 and was known as the City Widened Lines. A consequence of this operation was the remodelling of the Metropolitan Railway's King's Cross station and this pair of views, drawn at the time the station was enlarged, makes for an interesting comparison. The first is from the *Illustrated Times* of 29th February 1868 and the second from the *Illustrated London News*, 8th February 1868. The line at the left is the up track of the Great Northern and the next pair carry the up Midland and down Great Northern and Midland trains.

The *Illustrated Times*'s artist has incorrectly included mixed gauge track but has not been afraid to show the engineers' clutter not yet removed from the track side. Both views show the strange signal, which appears to be a temporary affair belonging to the contractors.

KING'S CROSS, as built 1863

This was the largest station of the original line, its overall roof sheltering four tracks, the pair on the right for Great Northern trains. The King's Cross Thameslink station of today stands on the site of the original Metropolitan station, although it displays none of the splendid architecture ascribed to the original structure. Of the latter was said:

> The station at King's-cross is a few feet below the surface of the road, and is a most elegant piece of work in every respect. There are two wide platforms; and spanning a width of about ninety feet, and sustained by girders of open work, is the station building itself, containing booking-offices, waiting-rooms, parcels-offices, &c., communicating with the platforms by stairs and landings in duplicate, one set serving for arrivals, the other for departures. The station is covered by an elliptical wrought-iron roof with sufficient glass to preserve an agreeable but not a glaring light, and is considered to be the handsomest station on the line. (Pinks, op. cit.)

The view opposite was drawn probably in the 1870s, after the broad gauge rails had been lifted. The separate entrance and exit galleries are visible, also a sign 'Wait here for Second Class'. Similar signs were placed to indicate where the first and third class carriages of the train would draw up.

> The exits from the stations are always separate from the entrances, which facilitates the separation of arriving passengers from those departing and avoids congestion on the staircases. (Troske L., 'Die Londoner Untergrundbahnen')

(Illustration from 'London Pictorially Described', London: Knapp, James B. undated)

THE UNDERGROUND STATION AT KING'S CROSS.

CLERKENWELL TUNNEL

It may sound remarkable today but the arrangements here were regarded as one of the wonders of the age when constructed. The book 'Old and New London' remarked 'the tunnel of the Midland and Great Northern lines is made to dive from north-east to south-west under that of the Metropolitan, which is here some thirty feet below the surface revealing the fact that "even in the lowest depths there is a lower still", and displaying one of the greatest triumphs of the engineer's art to be seen in the neighbourhood of London. This gigantic "tunnel under another tunnel" was carried into effect without the stoppage of a single train on the Metropolitan Railway.'

The illustration, from the *Illustrated London News* dated 8th February 1868 shows the criss-cross wrought iron girders of the bridge that carries the Metropolitan tracks over the City Widened Lines and gave rise to the name 'Grid-iron'. It was rebuilt (for the second time) in 1960, using reinforced concrete beams and slabs instead of iron girders, so its appearance is slightly different today. The centre-balanced arm signal suspended beneath the large arch was in accordance with early Metropolitan signalling practice.

But if the Metropolitan tunnel line under the streets of London is a striking, though familiar, fact; more remarkable still is it to find a tunnel under a tunnel under the streets of London. Yet so it is. When the traveller by the Midland Railway arrives at Kentish Town and proceeds to Moorgate Street, he passes under two railways at St. Pancras – one above the other – and soon finds himself at the King's Cross station, on the north side of the Metropolitan line. The train again starts, runs for a few minutes, and emerging from a tunnel, the traveller is now on the south side of the Metropolitan; in that short distance he has passed under the Underground … The Midland, the Great Northern, and the Dover and Chatham trains run from the King's Cross (Metropolitan) station, parallel with the original Metropolitan line proper for a distance of about 1,000 yards, they then descend by an incline of 1 in 100 until they have passed through a tunnel under the Metropolitan and then they rise by a steep slope 230 yards long of 1 in 40 (at one spot it is 1 in 39) up to Farringdon station; or, rather, three feet below the level of the Farringdon station of the Metropolitan proper. (Williams, F.S., op. cit.)

AERIAL VIEW OF THE VINE STREET AREA, 1868

In this remarkably well-detailed view of the area just west of Farringdon Street station there are several landmarks (the Metropolitan Tavern for instance) which have not altered in over a hundred years, although Turnmill Street is no longer quite the major artery of traffic it appears to have been in 1868. The smoking chimney arising from the cutting belongs to a pump-house which drained the railway here. The artist seems not to have accorded the Metropolitan locomotive its full complement of wheels; note too the characteristic rigid eight-wheel carriages with their false clerestories containing gas bags for illumination. The covered bridge in the foreground carries a sewer pipe. Two westbound trains appear to be waiting to start. (*Illustrated Times*, 29th February 1868)

FARRINGDON STREET, original station

Here a goods train, presumably Great Northern, approaches the original Farringdon Street terminus some time before opening. According to the late Ken Benest, who had studied plans of the station given in an accident report, the drawing is reasonably accurate. Behind the goods train is a carriage shed, the building on the right with roof lights is a small engine shed and the signal cabin is also visible. The artist appears to have omitted the third rail of the mixed gauge tracks and by comparison with an accident diagram of 25th March 1863, the drawing is somewhat deficient in terms of signalling and trackwork.

At the Farringdon-road station of the Metropolitan Railway, which is about one hundred yards from the foot of Holborn-hill, there are three platforms, two for passengers, and one for goods. Two of the lines which run into the station are doubled for the broad or narrow gauge, the other for the narrow gauge only. (Pinks, op. cit.)

FARRINGDON STREET, original station

Farringdon Street was the eastern terminus of the Metropolitan Railway but not for long. For this reason pictures of the original station are extremely scarce and for our best views we are dependent on a history book of Clerkenwell which just happened to balance its views of antiquity with the latest wonder of the age. Sited just off Victoria Street (later Farringdon Road), the location was also termed the Victoria Station in at least one pre-opening report (*London Journal*, vol. 35 (1862), p. 365).

This external view shows a rather austere building, probably built relatively cheaply, since it was envisaged as a temporary station only.

(Illustration from Pinks, op. cit.)

FARRINGDON STREET, new station interior

This is the station as rebuilt for through traffic. The classical architecture of the signal cabin is notable and, its disappearance apart, the rest of the fabric of the station has not changed much in the intervening years. The Great Northern train on the right is standing on the City Widened Lines tracks (now used by Thameslink).

The original caption notes:

> The immense development of traffic on the Metropolitan (or, as it is popularly known, the Underground) Railway, having received a further accession by its connection to the irrepressible London Chatham and Dover, the old station in Farringdon-road became inadequate to the public requirements and a new structure became necessary.

Accordingly the new station, a little up Farringdon-road, was erected and opened some weeks ago. One side of the station is devoted to the trains of the GNR with which the Metropolitan is connected at King's-cross and the other to the traffic of the Underground and the LC&D.

It is notable that the original station was not closed immediately, as the following report explained.

> The new station of the Metropolitan Railway, standing at the corner of Cow-cross and Turnmill-street, Clerkenwell, is removed but a few paces from Victoria-street (Farringdon-road), and is close behind that which has been known heretofore as the Farringdon-road station. It will hereafter, we understand, altogether supersede the latter which is now used merely for the Great Western and Kensington traffic.

(Illustration from *Illustrated Times*, 10th March 1866)

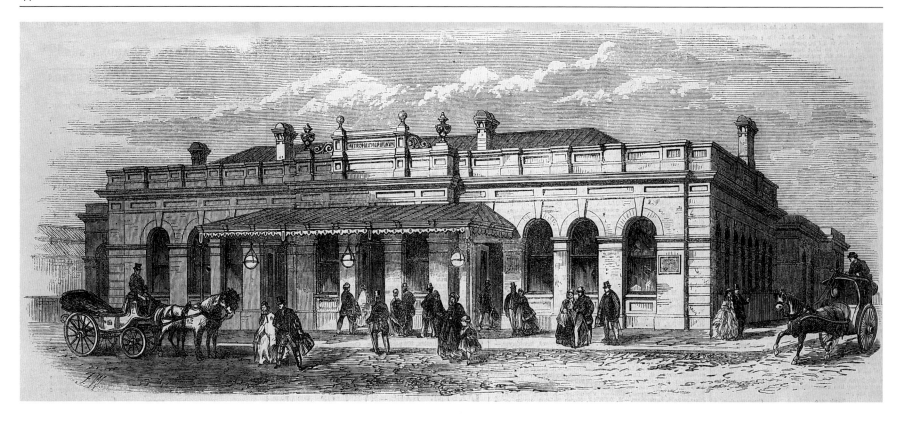

FARRINGDON STREET, new station

The new station of 23rd December 1865 was decidedly more elaborate than the structure it replaced. This building fronted what is now Cowcross Street just east of the temporary terminus. It was rebuilt in its present form in 1923. (*Illustrated London News*, 10th February 1866)

SMITHFIELD WEST JUNCTION (*Facing page*)

Here we have a well-observed view of the Farringdon 'C' signal cabin and the remarkable shell-arm signals. These latter were employed where two signalmen needed to exercise control over the same signal and were apparently so called from a fancied resemblance to a half-open bivalve. The signals combined the function of station (i.e. starting) signal of one cabin and distance (or indeed home) signal of the cabin in advance.

The original caption described the view as the Junction of the Metropolitan Railway and the London, Chatham and Dover Railway, although correctly speaking the junction known as West Street was an end-on connection about a hundred yards up the branch towards Snow Hill. The two tracks at the right now carry Thameslink services between stations north and south of the Thames. In this view they are shown to be protected by temporary timber work from falling debris during the construction of Smithfield Market.

The establishment, two or three weeks ago, of a continuous railway communication (though with a change of trains) between the Metropolitan Extension and London Chatham and Dover Railway on the south side of the Thames, and the Metropolitan or Underground Railway, which gives access to the Great Northern, Midland and Great Western lines in the northern and western districts of London, is a very important addition to our travelling facilities. The illustration we have engraved is a view of the junction, near Smithfield, the line of rails to the left hand being that by which trains coming from King's-cross go on to the City terminus of the Metropolitan Railway; while the line to the right hand is that by which trains may pass, through to the London Chatham and Dover Company at Ludgate-hill, where the passengers can either take the trains of the Metropolitan Extension to Brixton, Clapham, the Crystal Palace, or Pimlico; or may proceed towards Margate, Canterbury, or Dover by the main line.

(*Illustrated London News*, 27th January 1866)

THE JUNCTION OF THE LONDON, CHATHAM, AND DOVER RAILWAY WITH THE METROPOLITAN RAILWAY, NEAR SMITHFIELD.

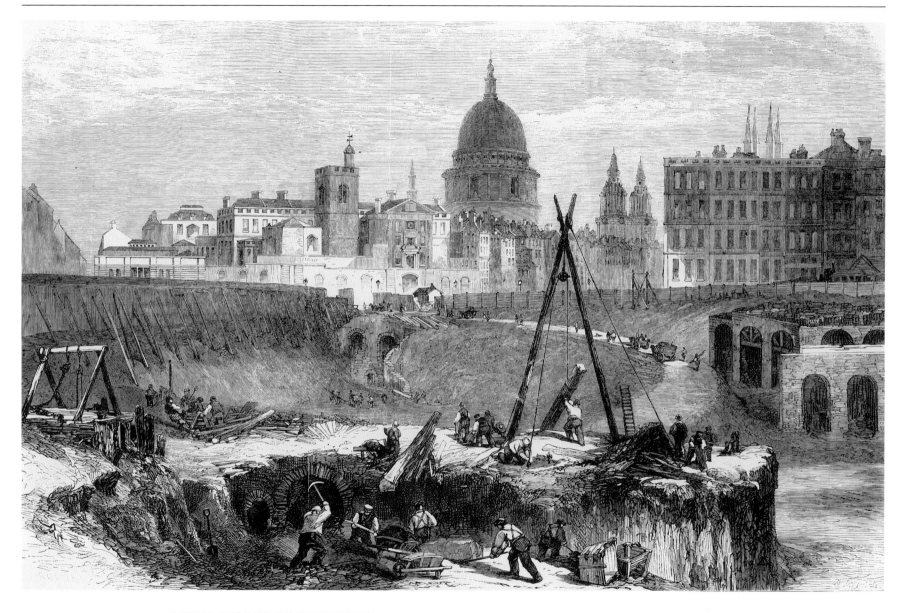

INITIAL WORKS AT SMITHFIELD

These two pictures depict construction of a later section of the line and show the kind of turmoil seen in the early stages of underground railway construction. At this stage, confusion is everywhere and the panorama gives little clue of the shape of future operations.

The viewpoint is near the bottom of Cowcross Street and St John Street, looking toward the south-west. Manual labour reigns supreme, with hoists, wheelbarrows and pickaxes. Note the deep excavations, exposing the cellar arches of demolished buildings.

The Engineer (30th January 1863) informed cheerily of this work: 'By passing through the north side of Smithfield it destroys a hideous nest of knackers' yards and slaughter-houses, blood refiners and glue and gut makers, who now combine to poison the air in this part of the city.'

The construction actually depicted here is the so-called Finsbury extension which took the line on from Farringdon Street onwards to Finsbury Circus (the eventual station was named Moorgate-street). While these works were in progress, the *Illustrated London News* wrote (on 17th December 1864): 'It appears, moreover, that the Metropolitan Extension will not stop at Finsbury but be continued to Liverpool-street, in the very heart of the City.'

(Illustration from *Illustrated London News*, 1st April 1865)

THE METROPOLITAN RAILWAY EXTENSION WORKS AT SMITHFIELD.—SEE PAGE 195.

Work has reached an advanced stage after about eight months of acitivity. The angle of the view is slightly different; the Post Office building seen at the left on the page opposite is now at the right of the picture. Engineers examine plans in the foreground as box girders of wrought iron to support the new market superstructure are beginning to be placed in position nearby. (Illustration from *Illustrated London News*, 2nd December 1865)

BUILDING A STATION

Aldersgate-street station was the first station on the extension beyond Farringdon-street to Moorgate-street.
Illustrations of stations under construction are less common, so this view is particularly welcome. Charterhouse Square
is seen at the left and Rayne Street is carried across the new railway in the foreground.

(Illustration from *Illustrated London News*, 2nd December 1865)

ALDERSGATE STREET, station exterior

The street corner situation of the station now called Barbican has not altered over the years but just about everything else has. It appears that the station building was designed with office or living accommodation above, something lacking in most other Metropolitan city stations. The overall roof of the trainshed can just be seen at the left. This was 380ft (116m) long with a span of 80ft (24m) covering three platforms and four tracks.

(Illustration from *Illustrated London News*, 10th February 1866)

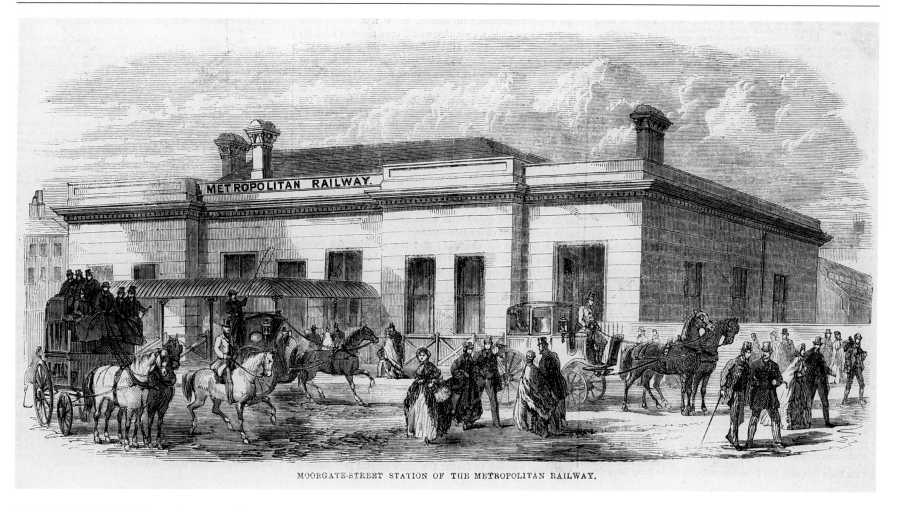

MOORGATE-STREET STATION OF THE METROPOLITAN RAILWAY.

MOORGATE STREET, station exterior

Much rebuilt since, this illustration gives an impression of the original, and rather plain, aspect of the Metropolitan's chief city station. An 80-bedroom hotel over the street level building here was proposed by Sir Edward Watkin when the line was extended to Liverpool Street and Aldgate in 1878, but investors showed no enthusiasm for this.

(Illustration from *Illustrated Times*, 10th March 1866)

ALDGATE TERMINUS (*Facing page*)

A composite interior/exterior view showing successfully the grand scale of a station which is so busy for a few hours of the day and almost lifeless the rest of the time. The lower picture looks south; its artist has done well in his depiction of the building but his impression of the locomotives and rolling stock is less impressive.

(Illustration from *Illustrated London News*, 2nd December 1876)

JUNCTION OF THE ST JOHN'S WOOD AND METROPOLITAN RAILWAYS AT BAKER STREET

This is the scene when work began on what was to become the Metropolitan Railway's main line, reaching far into Buckinghamshire. The double track tunnel curves east to join the original line just east of the 1863 Baker Street station. Train services between Moorgate Street and Swiss Cottage began on 13th April 1868.

PADDINGTON, PRAED STREET, exterior

This station, on the opposite side of the road to the Great Western terminus, was opened on 1st October 1868 with the extension to Gloucester Road. Part of the entrance canopy of the GWR's 1854 hotel can be seen at the extreme right. This view looking east shows the entrance to the station as well as the arch of its overall iron and glass roof, which emphasises how shallow the railway runs here. Subsequent rebuilding has disguised this effect.

(Illustration from *Illustrated London News*, 10th October 1868)

KENSINGTON

This is a very early view of High Street Kensington, which opened on 1st October 1868. At the time it was the only station for Kensington, as implied by the name boards, although South Kensington station followed a few weeks after on 24th December. Separate footbridges were provided for boarding and alighting passengers. The two tracks on the west side formed the Metropolitan District Railway's northern terminus.

(Illustration from *Illustrated London News*, 10th October 1868)

GLOUCESTER ROAD (*Facing page*)

A delightfully animated view of this station looking east with the District Railway's two tracks at the right. This is another of the stations provided with separate footbridges and staircases for boarding and alighting passengers. The illustration was found in an American book of 1888 by T. C. Clarke entitled 'The American Railway'.

WORKS AT WESTMINSTER

Views of the construction of the southern half of the Inner Circle are fairly uncommon, doubtless because coming a few years later, they were considered no longer of public interest. Either that or the Metropolitan District was less *au fait* with achieving press publicity. In any case, this illustration shows clearly the significant level of demolition required to achieve the new line of route.

In the construction of the tunnel between Westminster Bridge and the St James's Park Stations, great difficulties presented themselves from the irregular nature of the soil, but these were in the end surmounted; and in the course of the excavations at this point quantities of bones of animals – supposed to be those of the mammoth and other antediluvian creatures – were unearthed. Another difficulty arose from the fear of the excavations weakening the foundations of the Abbey. The line passes almost close under the wall of St Margaret's Church and Westminster Abbey, and emerges into daylight close by Queen Anne's Gate, near the St James's Park Station. (Walford, op. cit.)

(Illustrations from the author's collection, source of drawing unknown)

PARLIAMENT SQUARE EXCAVATED.

Cut and cover works are at an early stage in this view, which looks north east. The digging up of Parliament Square was not allowed 130 years later, when the Jubilee Line extension was built nearby.

CONSTRUCTION WORKS ON THE THAMES EMBANKMENT AT WESTMINSTER

An easy view to identify is this one, immediately north of the Houses of Parliament. The railway being built here is the Metropolitan District and its construction coincided conveniently with that of Sir Joseph Bazalgette's Victoria Embankment, itself a major improvement work. A later report in the *Illustrated London News* (25th June 1870) described the 'magnificent new carriage road along the Embankment, with its broad foot pavements along each side; beneath which runs the Low-Level Sewer on the one hand and the Metropolitan District Railway on the other. The exterior face of the Embankment, towards the river, presents a massive granite wall, ornamented with colossal lions' heads in bronze, similar to the western sections from the Temple to Waterloo, and from Waterloo to Westminster Bridge, which have so grand an appearance.'

(Illustration from *Illustrated London News*, 6th November 1869)

THE THAMES EMBANKMENT, adjacent to Charing Cross

If this sectional view looks familiar, that's because it is sometimes chosen to illustrate articles on the uncompleted Waterloo and Whitehall Railway. It also gives us an impression of the general appearance of this part of London 133 years ago. The South Eastern Railway's 1864 terminus at Charing Cross with its approach over Hungerford Bridge is seen in the background. The numbered exhibits are

1. Pipe subway
2. Low-level sewer
3. Metropolitan District Railway
4. The Pneumatic Railway (Waterloo & Whitehall Rly).

(Illustration from *Illustrated London News*, 16th March 1867)

The book 'The World of Wonders' (1877) informs us:

Between Blackfriars and the Temple stations the line (here, as in other parts, covered in by a system of girders and flat brick arches) passes over numerous sewers, which discharge into the low-level intercepting sewer lying on the left between the railway and the river. All these tributary sewers had to be, as it were, flattened or rather, reconstructed with flat tops, so as to allow the rails to be laid at a proper level. Above, of course, are the Embankment and its gardens, and within the precincts of the Temple the train passes over a sub-stratum of six inches of tan, in order that its passage may disturb as little as possible the abstruse legal studies of the tenants of the adjoining chambers. Thence, passing under one of the arches of Waterloo Bridge, where, before the Embankment was constructed, the muddy foreshore of the river lay, the line proceeds to Charing Cross and Westminster stations, the latter having a subway communicating direct with the Houses of Parliament.

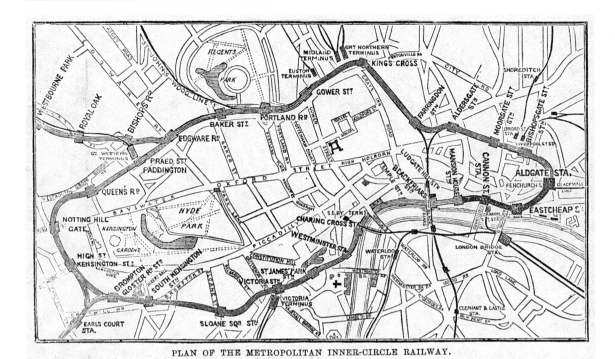

PLAN OF THE METROPOLITAN INNER-CIRCLE RAILWAY.

Facing page Tunnel construction under temporary wooden shoring is being carried out by the light of naked gas flares.

Left Map showing the last section of the Inner-Circle (in heavy black ink), construction of which was completed on 6th October 1884.

THE METROPOLITAN INNER-CIRCLE RAILWAY

The Metropolitan District Railway Company, two months since, gave formal possession of land adjoining the Mansion House station to the Inner Circle Completion Company, in order to enable them to commence the necessary works for the new or link line from that point to the Metropolitan Railway near the present Aldgate station, and so to surround Inner London with a continuous circle. The Act for the link line was first obtained in 1874, but in consequence of various obstacles which interfered with the commencement of the undertaking, a second Act was passed in 1876 to extend the time originally granted. It is under this second Act that the works are now put in hand, and they must be completed within two years from Aug. 7 last.

Beginning at the Mansion House station, the new line will follow Queen Victoria-street as far as Cannon-street, and thence will pass under Cannon-street to the point where King William-street, Gracechurch-street, and Eastcheap meet. Here it turns to the north, passing under buildings which will be taken down, and falls into Fenchurch-street between Rood-lane and Cullum-street. It then follows the line of Fenchurch-street to a point a few yards eastward of the site of Old Aldgate Pump, and from there turns northwards, passing under Houndsditch to unite with the Metropolitan Railway by the Cloth Exchange. After leaving the Mansion House station, the first new station will be at Cannon-street, between Walbrook and St. Swithin's-lane, to allow of interchange of traffic with the South-

Eastern Railway. The next will be at the corner of Gracechurch-street and Eastcheap, on the site of the National Provident Institution, and the third in Aldgate, at a point between the site of the Old Pump and Jewry-street. From the Eastcheap station to Fenchurch-street a new street will be made above the railway; and this street, for which the Metropolitan Board of Works and the Commissioners of Sewers have undertaken to pay half a million sterling, will be three sixteenths of a mile long, measuring from the statue in Aldgate; and it is further expected that communications will be made with the passenger lines at the Fenchurch-street station.

While active preparations are being made for the completion of the Inner Circle, the directors of the District Railway are carrying out works at the other end of their system which promise to be of great utility. They have lately opened direct lines to Hammersmith and to Richmond, and they are now about to pass from Hammersmith over the South-Western rails as far as Turnham-green, and thence by a new line of their own to Ealing. By this arrangement, passengers from Ealing will be admitted directly, and without change of carriages, to all the metropolitan stations of the District system, and will thus be brought within easy reach of Charing-cross, the Temple, and the Mansion House. With a view to the probable requirements of this traffic, the lines in the vicinity of Earl's Court are being altered and simplified, and other improvements are in progress in various parts of the line.

Illustrated London News, 17th November 1877

Traffic levels rapidly exceeded expectations and overcrowding was inevitable at times. This view of a Metropolitan station on the Oxford and Cambridge boat race day shows the staff battling to contain the crowds at a station which is probably Baker Street but could be Portland Road or Gower Street. The natural lighting ducts are apparent, also the 'Wait Here for First Class' sign (of little use under these conditions!).

THE VICTORIAN TRAVEL EXPERIENCE

Without a time machine we cannot really experience the atmosphere of a trip on the Inner Circle more than a hundred years ago – or can we? Here is a selection of impressions of travellers and other observers which seemed well worthy of saving from obscurity. (Illustration from *Illustrated London News*, 23rd March 1872)

A pleasant experience?

It is clear that the Metropolitan and Metropolitan District Railways soon fell victim to their own success. Although one of the aims of building an underground railway was to relieve traffic congestion and pressure on existing modes of transport, the overcrowding was soon transferred below, as the illustration above shows.

Not only was overcrowding frequent, lack of ventilation caused further problems.

There are 13 miles of the Inner Circle railway and in this distance occur more than double that number of stations. Some of these are more underground than others. But the ventilation was found to be very defective; complaints of the gas were heard from all stations; the glass was removed and the air permitted access. Some of the stations are planted in cuttings and plenty of ventilation is secured. ('Triumphs of Modern Engineering', c. 1900)

One part of the line remained in which the foul air continued to cause annoyance and discomfort to the passengers. This extended from the Portland Road to the Gower Street station. Between these stations the arch of the tunnel is crossed nearly at right angles by the tube of the old Pneumatic Despatch company. In a lucky moment the 'happy thought' arose that this tube might be made subservient to the removal of the foul air in the tunnel beneath, and the more efficient ventilation of the railway in its immediate vicinity. In 1874 this idea was most successfully worked out and practically applied. (Walford, op. cit.)

Newspaper reports of the offensive atmosphere of the London Underground were numerous and they reached far beyond these shores. Benson Bobrick, in his book 'Labyrinths of Iron' (New York: Newsweek Books, 1981), quotes three undated reports in American publications which make dramatic reading.

New Yorkers could read the lurid first-hand reports of a correspondent like Francis Kirk, writing in the *Scientific American*: 'What is at first merely unpleasant soon becomes unhealthy and eventuates in a subtle poison, first affecting delicate organizations, and afterwards visiting alike the weak and the strong, the unhealthy and the healthy, engendering pestilence, and this is the ready ally of all contagious diseases. Surely such a calamity should not be visited upon any people under cover of an enactment for their benefit.'

One day the New York *Post* announced: 'A coroner's jury has just condemned the atmosphere of the underground railway.' The jury convened to look into the death at King's Cross Station, London, of a woman named Dobrier attributed her death to a bronchial ailment accelerated by 'suffocating air.'

The New York *Tribune* carried an expanded account, sensationally italicised:

A young woman, apparently in *good health*, entered the Bishop's Road station on Wednesday evening. On reaching the platform she said; 'It is a very nice station but very hot.' On getting into one of the carriages she said: '*What a dreadful smell there is here.*' These were the last words she spoke! At King's Cross she was taken out by her companion in apparently lifeless condition. A physician being sent for, arrived in five minutes, and found her *dead*. An examination showed she had died from restriction of the aortic orifice.

An inquiry showed 'that sulphurous and carburetted gases [had] gone on accumulating in the tunnels of the railway till the air had become dangerous to breathe, till the presence of choke damp, to be followed by fire damp, threatened a terrible explosion.' Occasional passengers complain of *headaches, sulphurous taste on the palate, and a stinging sensation in the throat, as of common occurrence. The employees at the station complain of the air, affirming that no man whose lungs are delicate can keep at work without suffering, and that a short dry, hacking cough is common among all who are on duty.* At the first inquest the *coroner declared* that he avoided the railway as much as possible, *because of the depressing effect he experienced from the confined atmosphere.* The jury returned a verdict, in the words of the surgeon, that: DEATH WAS ACCELERATED BY THE SUFFOCATING ATMOSPHERE OF THE UNDERGROUND RAILWAY.

RAILWAY ACCIDENT AT EARL'S-COURT STATION

On Sunday afternoon at three o'clock, a disaster by which two men were killed took place at the Earl's-court station of the Metropolitan District Railway, West Brompton. A train of the Great Western Railway Company had just left that station, on its way to the Addison-road station and the Westbourne Park junction. At the same time, a train from Putney to Whitechapel was approaching to enter the Earl's-court station. The signalling apparatus at the Warwick-road junction was out of order, as it is supposed, from some derangement of the connecting-rod; hence the signal duly given did not act, and the driver of the Putney train believed the line to be clear. The two trains moving in opposite directions, though neither of them was going at speed, came into direct collision, the two engines striking each other with great force. They were smashed and locked together as they lay on the line, while the foremost carriage of the Great Western train was lifted and thrown on top of its engine. The engine-driver, John Davison, had a portion of the carriage falling on his leg, which was terribly crushed; he was removed to St. George's Hospital, but died in a few hours. The stoker of this train, Thomas Simmonds, was also mortally injured, dying in the same hospital next day. The guards of the Great Western train escaped, and none of the passengers were seriously hurt; but, in the Putney train, one passenger, Mr. Sladden, of Putney, suffered internal injuries which may have very bad consequences; he was taken to the hospital. Our illustration, from a sketch by Mr. Godfrey Merry, shows the scene of the accident immediately after it occurred.

(*Illustrated London News*, 29th August 1885)

This collision actually took place at Warwick Road Junction signal box. Despite the heavy traffic handled, only one passenger was killed on the District Railway (at Hammersmith Junction in 1876) up to the time it was absorbed into London Transport in 1933. The Metropolitan Railway, even more intensively used, had no train accidents fatal to passengers in its first 44 years of operation.

PORTLAND ROAD

Our final illustration for this station is not without charm. It is a lithograph from a children's book and whilst it may be simplistic, it certainly embodies the atmosphere of the station in a realistic manner.

> Wonderful trains! From morn till night,
> Clattering through tunnels without daylight,
> Hither and thither they run, up and down,
> Beneath the streets of London Town.
>
> Many prefer these trains instead
> Of the cabs and 'Busses' overhead,
> For they run much faster than horses can,
> Miss Dot's papa is a busy man,
>
> And goes to the City every day
> By the 'Underground,' – the quickest way;
> And One Hundred Millions of people, 't is found,
> Are carried each year by the 'Underground.'

The original spelling and punctuation have been retained, as elsewhere in this book.

('London Town' by Thomas Crane and Ellen Houghton; London: Marcus Ward & Co., 1883)

PENNY GUIDE

This splendid Gothic style cover was used for a number of editions of the Metropolitan Railway Illustrated Guide published by Morton & Company of Queen Victoria Street in the late nineteenth century. Apart from the description of the railway itself, reproduced opposite, details were given of places of interest on or near the line of route.

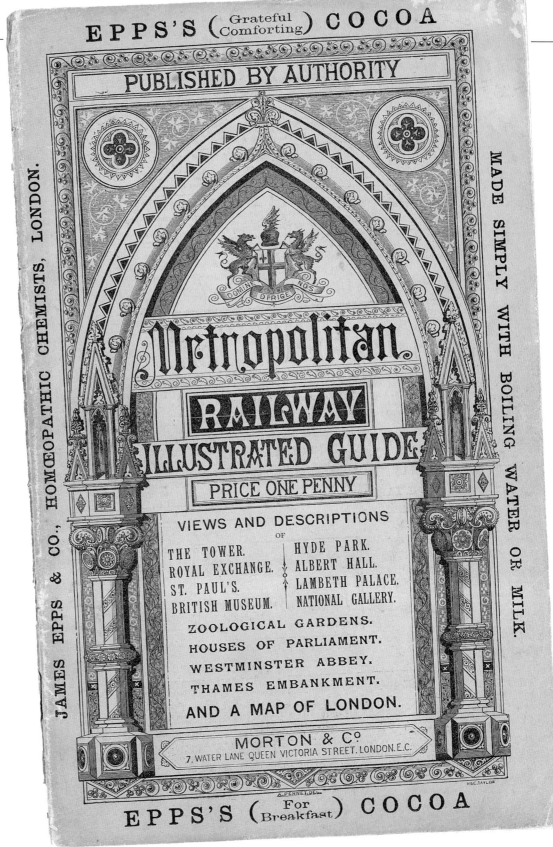

UNDERGROUND

THE construction of the Metropolitan Railway illustrates very vividly the density of London life, and the mode in which engineers have grappled with the difficulty. To run a line from Paddington into the City three courses were open. One was to choose the road level, and thus practically block all other traffic. This was obviously inadmissible. A second was to construct it on pillars level with the first floor windows as in New York, or on brick arches similar to that of the Blackwall line. Both these ideas were not only expensive but open to many other objections. A third course remained, which was to run beneath the level. This was finally adopted and received in common parlance the title of "The Underground." The original idea has been largely extended, and that which at the outset was a mere branch from Paddington to Farringdon Street, now runs from Aldgate, through Paddington, to Hammersmith and Richmond, and through Notting Hill Gate, Kensington, and Westminster, to the Mansion House Station, forming the completion of the inner circle. At first sight few things could look so little needed as a Guide to the Metropolitan Railway, yet in reality there are few lines in England where such information is more essentially necessary. It may be pointed out that almost all the great railways which have termini in London, either have running powers over some portion of the system, or are placed in direct relationship with it. To make this clear, it will be better to mention the more salient points connected with each station. The present terminus of the Metropolitan Railway is at Aldgate, which is the station nearest to the Docks, the Tower of London, and the Fenchurch Street Station of the Blackwall Railway, from which ready access can be obtained to any of the eastern parts of London. The next station is that of Bishopsgate : here are the termini of the Great Eastern Railway and the North London Railway. Passing onward the next station is that of Moorgate Street ; here several of the larger railways have booking offices, and their trains run into this station. These railways are the London, Chatham, and Dover, the Midland, the Great Northern, and the Great Western. Passengers can book through to any station on their respective lines. Aldersgate Street Station is the next, and is the point nearest for St. Paul's Cathedral, the General Post Office, and the locality of the general Manchester trade. The next station is that of Farringdon Street, near to which is the Holborn Viaduct and Newgate. One step further on is King's Cross, where the junction is formed with the Great Northern and Midland Railways ; whilst Gower Street is the point nearest to the British Museum, and also the station nearest to Euston, the main terminus of the London and North Western Railway. After which we arrive at Portland Road for Regent's Park, and Baker Street for St. John's

Wood, where passengers have to leave their carriages and pass over the bridge into the St. John's Wood Railway Station, the line of which is now extended to Harrow. The next station is Edgware Road, the great junction of the line, for here the train sweeps either to the right or the left ; if to the right then through Bishop's Road Station to the Hammersmith branch. At this point the Metropolitan Railway joins the Great Western line (the main terminus of which is at Paddington), and passes onward through Westbourne Park, Notting Hill, and Hammersmith, to Kew Gardens and Richmond. At Notting Hill there is a junction with the middle route for Addison Road, Kensington, whence the line continues to Gloucester Road Station, rejoining the Inner Circle or main line at that point. To complete the Inner Circle it is necessary to return to Edgware Road. After starting, the train sweeps to the left at the junction and passes through Praed Street, Notting-Hill Gate, South Kensington, and Westminster, to the Mansion House, which is the terminal station on this part of the route. In a rough way this indicates the grouping and connection of the Metropolitan Railway, the more specific details of stations and the points of interest which are nearest to them are given at page 40. Special care has been taken to protect passengers from mistakes, by placing at each station a notice board, on which is indicated the destination of every train before it enters the station. We turn from these matters of detail to point out that the Metropolitan Railway runs through a district that in certain respects has no equal in the world. No capital can boast of parks equal to Hyde Park and Kensington Gardens. No museums equal our South Kensington and British Museums, in fulness of resource, untold wealth, and abundance of example. No gallery combines the same groundwork of scientific teaching and artistic treasure, illustrating alike the past and the present, as our own National Gallery. More splendid paintings illustrative of particular schools, or particular men, occur in almost every gallery of note in Europe, but in its combined aspect it may challenge any that can be named. It has risen out of chaos, and has before it a splendid future In a somewhat similar sense the surroundings of Westminster Abbey are absolutely unique. No other spot exists where the most illustrious examples of the past are entwined so closely with the virile life of the present, while in mere architectural beauty it can fairly hold its own. No one would compare London with Paris so far as mere beauty is concerned, yet on our Thames Embankments there are phases of grouping which will vie with the most superb points of view of the Paris Quays. All these localities, with numberless others, lie on the route of the Metropolitan Railway. Those who want to see London should remember that, like all great cities, its objects of attraction and interest are endless ; they grow out of every struggle and are increased by every epoch. Yet in a rough way there are not above a dozen special sights whose reputation is world-wide, and all of these can be readily reached by the Underground Railway.

PORTABLE READING LIGHTS

Early publicity pronouncements, such as this one soon after the opening, made grand claims for the standard of lighting in carriages:

> The plan of lighting carriages by gas has, up to the present, been found to work admirably both as regards economy and power of illumination. The gas reservoirs on the roof of each carriage can be filled from the stand-pipes in two minutes and a half, and one filling lasts for nearly three hours. (*The Engineer*, 30th January 1863)

Perhaps more attention was paid to economy since it soon became clear that illumination was not all it might have been . . .

> The question of providing a greater amount of light in railway carriages has for years past occupied the attention of railway managers, but a pardonable solicitude for the company's purse has prevented most of them from effecting such an improvement as would silence the constantly repeated complaints of their passengers. It is true that on many lines gas has superseded oil, but the increased illumination is scarcely more than was required to enable the passenger to enter and leave the train in safety, while the possibility of reading in comfort is still out of the question.
>
> An increased roof light, moreover, is scarcely what is wanted by the travelling public, as the passenger who desires to read requires a separate light near his book. To the Metropolitan District Railway Company belongs the credit of being the first to adopt a system of electric lighting which supplies this want, and which, while it does not call for any expenditure of capital by the railway company, gives the travelling public just what is wanted, and at the same time admits of a satisfactory profit being made by the company undertaking the supply. This want is met by the railway electric reading lamp, which is a machine invented by Mr. Tourtel for retailing electric light to passengers by pennyworths.
>
> A few of these lamps have been experimentally in use on the Metropolitan District Railway for the past two years, and the results of the trials have been so satisfactory that a contract has been made by that company with the Railway Electric Reading Lamp Company to install up to 10,000 reading lamps in the carriages of the District Railway. It is not intended at present to displace the gas lamps in use in the roofs of carriages, but to provide a separate light for passengers desiring to read.
>
> Upon introducing a penny into the slot at the top of the machine and subsequently pressing a knob, an electric light, which is of about 3-candle power in strength, is obtained which burns for about half an hour, at the end of which time it is automatically extinguished, but can be relighted by the insertion of another penny.
>
> (Original document quoted in Maurice Rickards' book 'New Inventions', London: Hugh Evelyn, 1969)

TOURTEL'S APPLIANCE FOR PROVIDING LIGHT BY THE PENNYWORTH.

First class

Third class

THE PATENT
NEXT STATION INDICATOR

It is only in the last decade that London Underground has introduced electronic 'next station' indicators aboard trains and commercial sponsorship of some of its travel information, but of course there is nothing new under the sun. In fact both of these developments were already combined 100 years ago with a mechanical device provided in every compartment of some coaches.

A colourful description is found in an article entitled Underground London in the *Windsor Magazine* (issue VI, 1897) in which the narrator's curiosity is relieved by an inspector of the railway company.

I had always thought it part of the guard's duty to work these indicators, for sometimes the indicator may pass over several flaps before it stops at the right one, and it seemed to me this must be done by human agency. The inspector put me right.

'No, it's much simpler than that,' said he. 'There's a flap of wood sticking up between the lines, soon after the train leaves any station, and this strikes a spring on the bottom of each carriage as they pass over, and this sends the indicator round. When some stations belonging to a branch line have to be missed out, there are three or four of these, as many as are wanted, in a row.'

'But it must be exceedingly difficult to arrange.'

'Yes, I suppose so. If they answer, we're going to have them on all the District lines.'

'Soon?'

'Yes, soon; but they won't be all round the Circle, you know, because the Metropolitan haven't taken to them.'

'And how can you tell if they answer?'

'It is part of the guard's duty to report. There have been very few failures so far – hardly any. They come expensive at first, of course, but the advertisements have helped to pay.'

It was realised early on that underground travellers represented a captive audience for advertising. In his book 'The Underground Story' (London: Robert Hale Ltd, 1963), Hugh Douglas writes:

Posters on the Underground are as old as the railway itself; in fact the wooden walls enclosing the works when the Metropolitan was being built, and even the stays supporting these walls, exhorted Londoners to see Blondin at the Crystal Palace, to read the *Clerkenwell News*, and to vote for Cox in the elections then being held. In the expanding Britain into which the Metropolitan was born, advertising proved a fruitful source of revenue, so shortly after the line opened the board of directors accepted a tender from Mr James Willing, granting him the right to sell newspapers and the right to handle all the advertising for a period of five years at a cost of £1,150 a year.

Advertising on the Underground grew rapidly from Mr Willing's £1,150 a year sideline. In fact, by the turn of the century advertising was so much a part of the railway of Britain that W. Gunn Gwennett, himself an illustrator of railway advertisements, was able to complain not only of their poor quality but of their large numbers.

'So thickly placarded are the stations of the Underground railway that it is no uncommon thing to hear two countrymen arguing whether they have arrived at Vinolia or Willing,' he wrote. 'An attempt has been made to remedy this by fitting some trains with a device which, after ringing a bell, shows a plate bearing the name of the next station. But the greater part of each plate is occupied by an advertisement so that here again the provincial or foreigner might suppose the name of the next station to be Vinolia as easily as Aldgate.'

FINDING ONE'S WAY

Several contemporary guides bear witness to the fact that orientation on the Underground was not as easy as it might have been. Here are some extracts from books of the period, commencing with 'Old London Street Cries'.

There are twenty-seven stations on the London Inner Circle Railway – owned by two companies, the Metropolitan and District – and the name of one only – Gower Street – is usually pronounced by 'that tchung men', the railway porter, as other people pronounce it. 'Emma Smith' (Hammersmith), while not a main line station, may be cited here as a good example of Cockney, for 'Arry and 'Arriet are quite incapable of any other verbal rendering. They are cried as follows:

South Kenzint'nn

Glawster Rowd

I Street Kenzint'nn

Nittin' Ill Gite (*ite* as in *flight*)

Queen's Rowd Bizewater (*ize* as in *size*)

Pride Street, Peddinten

Edge-wer Rowd (by common consent the
    Cockney refrains from saying Hedge-wer.)

Biker Street

Portland Rowd

Gower Street

King's Krauss (often abbreviated to Krauss)

Ferrinden Street

Oldersgit Street (no preliminary *H*)

Mawgit Street

Bish-er-git

Ol'git

Mark Line

Monneym'nt

Kennun Street

Menshun Ouse

Bleckfriars

Tempull (pull-pull-Tempull)

Chairin' Krauss

Wes'minster (One sometimes hears
    Wes'minister: a provincialism)

S'n Jimes-is Pawk (*ime s* in *time*)

Victaw-ia

Slown Square (*own* as in *town*)

Country cousins may be reminded that the guiding letters I or O so boldly marked on the tickets issued on the London underground railway, and, in the brightest vermilion, as conspicuously painted up in the various stations, do not mean 'Inner' or 'Outer' Circle, but the inner and outer lines of rails of the Inner Circle Railway. Though sanctioned by Parliament more than twenty years ago, the so-called Outer Circle Railway is still incomplete, its present form being that of a horse-shoe, with termini at Broad Street and Mansion House, and some of its principal stations at Dalston, Willesden and Addison Road, Kensington.

(Tuer, 'Old London Street Cries', 1885).

GETTING ABOUT

Here is a handy description of train services:

> Trains run on the 'inner circle' in both directions from 5.30 a.m. to nearly midnight, at intervals of 3–10 min. during the day, and of 20 min. before 7 a.m. or after 9 p.m. On Sundays the train-service is suspended during the 'church interval' (11 a.m.–1 p.m.).
>
> The stations generally occupy open sites, and are lighted from above, many of them being roofed with glass. The carriages are lighted with gas or electricity. The booking-office is generally on a level with the street, at the top of the flight of stairs leading down to the railway. The official who checks the tickets points out the right platform, while the tickets themselves are marked with a large red O or I (for 'outer' and 'inner' line of rails), corresponding with notices in the stations. After reaching the platform, the traveller had better enquire whether the train for his destination is the first that comes up or one of those that follow, or consult the somewhat inconspicuous telegraph-board on which the destination of the 'next train' is indicated. The terminus towards which the train is travelling is also generally placarded on the front of the engine. Above the platforms hang boards indicating the points at which the different classes of carriage are drawn up; the first-class carriages are in the middle of the train. The names of the stations are called out by the porters, and are always painted at different parts of the platform and on the lamps and benches, though frequently difficult to distinguish from the surrounding advertisements. As the stoppages are extremely brief, no time should be lost either in taking seats or alighting. Passengers leave the platform by the 'Way Out', where their tickets are given up. Those who are travelling with through-tickets to a station situated on one of the branch-lines show their tickets at the junction where carriages are changed, and where the officials will indicate the proper train. – Compare the time-tables of the companies.
>
> The carriages are of three classes; the third class is apt to be inconveniently crowded between 8 and 10 a.m. and 5 and 7 p.m. by passengers going to or returning from their daily work. The fares are extremely moderate, seldom exceeding a shilling even for considerable distances. Return-tickets are issued at a fare and a half. At first, in order to make himself acquainted with the Metropolis, the stranger will naturally prefer to make use of omnibuses and cabs, but when his early curiosity is satisfied he will probably often avail himself of the easy, rapid, and economical mode of travelling afforded by the Underground Railway. ('Baedeker's Handbook for London', 1905)

By telegraph-board the compiler presumably meant the type of platform indicator where one of a number of semaphore arms painted with destinations can be made to appear beneath a fixed 'next Train' board by pulling the appropriate lever. These devices were still to be found at a number of Southern Region stations in the London area until recently.

ORGANISATION OF STATIONS

Another delightful clarification of arrangements at stations:

> Tickets are overprinted with a large red-brown I or O. The same letters are made visible at or over the respective entrances and staircases: namely I at the entrance to Inner Rail platforms and O for the Outer Rail. Where a single entrance is provided (High Street) one enquires from an official which staircase to use. Only at King's Cross (Inner Rail) and a few other places is this provision not observed; the former is served by trains of several administrations and the traffic is thus more complex.
>
> To indicate the correct train small train indicators are provided at some stations on the platform close to the entrance. They are formed of small signs fixed about 2 metres high showing the destination station of the next train. Above is the wording **Train For**. Following the departure of the train another board becomes visible, being operated by the official responsible for checking tickets. The boards normally remain in the upper part of the case and become visible through a glass panel.
>
> To further aid the passenger find the carriage corresponding to his class of ticket there are signs on the Metropolitan Railway and the lines that it shares with the District Railway with the wording.
>
> Wait Here For
Third Class
>
> (or Second or First Class, respectively) suspended above the corresponding part of the platform. Earlier (in 1866) these signs hung high over the tracks such that they were not always clearly read; their current (1892) form with white letters on a dark blue background seems to fit their purpose well. The District Railway does not use these markers. Since the trains always stop at almost exactly the same spot and as a rule have the same formation of carriages, passengers using these signs can find their place before the arrival of the train. In this way chasing after trains is minimised, which is important because station stops are tightly measured amounting to only 20 seconds or so. Moreover the carriages are often well occupied and frequently over-full. (Troske, op. cit.)

SELECT BIBLIOGRAPHY

Sources and further reading

One of the joys of research is serendipity, the fortunate discovery of valuable information by accident. One of the most detailed contemporary descriptions of the construction of the Metropolitan Railway is found as a lengthy digression in William J. Pinks's *The History of Clerkenwell* (London, 1865).

Another superbly comprehensive and richly illustrated book (albeit in German) is *Die Londoner Untergrundbahnen* (=The London Underground Railways) by L. Troske (Berlin, 1892).

The best selection of early photographs is an album of 43 photographic views of work in progress dated July 1863. Entitled *London Metropolitan Railway* and generally known as the Fowler album, this book is to be found in the Guildhall Library London under the reference L48.5.

A similar collection of photographs is in *Building the Inner Circle Railway*, with accompanying text published by *The Railway Gazette* as a booklet of 32 pages in 1946.

Some attractive illustrations are to be found in the French book *Les Nouvelles Conquêtes de la Science* by G.L. Figuier (Paris, various undated editions). Very much a popular book, it does however include interesting details such as the fact that large gasometers were established at Bishopsgate and Mansion House to enable the carriage lighting cylinders to be refilled in just two minutes.

The book *Old And New London* by Walter Thornbury (London: Cassell & Company, 1897) is probably the most comprehensive popular history of London ever compiled. Richly illustrated with woodcuts, it runs to six volumes (plus a further two entitled *Greater London*) and saw many editions in the late 19th century. It is a rich source for all later historians and contains plenty of contemporary information about the capital's public works.

Finally, the equally definitive work on the history of the Metropolitan Railway is *London's Metropolitan Railway* by Alan A. Jackson (Newton Abbot: David & Charles, 1986).

Other books used as sources of illustrations are credited in the appropriate captions.

Finally, to savour the best evocation of this era in general I cannot recommend too highly *The London Doré Saw* by Eric de Maré [London: Allen Lane, 1973]. Taking as source material the same kind of engravings as this book does, the author conjures up an extremely powerful vision of mid-Victorian life and society. A marvellous book.

Articles in periodicals

Descriptions of the travel experience

'When the Circle was Steam Operated', by Fred T. Jane, pp. 133–137 + 150, *Railway Magazine*, May/June 1944, reprinted from the original article in the *English Illustrated Magazine*, August 1893.

'Underground London: A chat about its Railways', by G.E. Mitton and Wilfrid Klickmann, pp. 672–689, *Windsor Magazine*, volume VI, 1897.

History

'Genesis of the Underground', by C.H. Freeman, pp. 545–549, *Back Track*, October 1995.

'The Metropolitan in its Prime', by Charles E. Lee, pp. 93–102, *Railway Magazine*, February 1963.

Early locomotives

'Fowler's Ghosts', by Michael Robbins, pp. 390–394, *Railway Magazine*, June 1963.

'Facts and Fables of Fowler's Ghost', by Steamologist, pp. 18–22, *Railway World*, January 1974 and pp. 60–65 February 1974.

'Impressions of a Ghost', by Ian Huntley, pp. 134–138, *Railway World*, March 1988.

'Fowler's Ghost', by Peter Bloomfield, pp. 244–248, *Journal of the Historical Model Railway Society*.

'Borrowed Locomotives on the Metropolitan', by Charles E. Lee, pp. 582–585, *Railway Magazine*, July 1964.

Signalling

'Underground Signalling in the Steam Days', by T.S. Lascelles, pp. 102–104, *Railway Magazine*, March–April 1945.